Luck is not
a
Butterfly

Tine Thevenin

Also by Tine Thevenin:

The Family Bed: An Age-Old Concept In Childrearing
Lake Harriet
When Mama Was A Little Girl

Crossing The Finish Line (audio cassette tape)

Cover design and illustrations by Kim Ellin

Library of Congress Catalog Card Number: 88-90193
Thevenin, Tine
    Luck is not a butterfly
    1. Title

ISBN 0-960-2010-2-5

Printed in the United States of America
Burgess Printing Company
Minneapolis, Minnesota

Dedication

*To my mother and especially my father
who told me once, when I was a
little girl, "You will always
have luck."*

Acknowledgements

This is an anthology of my thoughts originally put down in my journal covering a time span of fifteen years. Anthology comes from two Greek words, "anthos "which means "flowers "and "legein" which means "to gather." Over the years, many people have added their flowers to my bouquet. In the actualy production of this book, however, I give special thanks to Dr. Kären Hess, who gave unselfishly of her editorial expertise, to Dag Knudsen for his continual supportive quest for excellence, and to Kim Ellin for her enthusiasm and artistic skills.

Each thought is like a seed,
Its potential enormous.

Life is a surprise package that holds untold mysteries to be discovered - things which are exciting, interesting, intriguing, awe-ful, awe-some, beautiful, inspiring. I am that surprise package. The world is that surprise package. And it excites me to open it wrap by wrap and discover what's inside to marvel at.

I heard a cardinal today. And while I was hanging out the wash, two pheasants flew overhead.

I firmly believe that it is going to rain only if you stay home. I've seldom been proven wrong even if we left in a downpour. Now, apply that lesson to all of life!

LUCK IS NOT A BUTTERFLY

A butterfly aimlessly flits about and by chance lands upon this flower or that one. A butterfly is difficult to catch, and only if you wait long enough with an outstretched hand may one, perhaps, come to you. But luck, that you may hold in your hands when you choose, for it does not come to you by chance. You look for it and find it. And once you have discovered how to find luck, you will have discovered a gold mine, serendipity, a ray of sunshine on even the dreariest of days.

To hold luck in your hands makes you a happy person. We would all like to have luck in our lives because to have good luck is a very exciting thing. Suppose, for instance, that you are walking down the street and suddenly, out of the corner of your eye, you see something flutter. You take a second look and what you see is money, a bill. You bend over and pick up the money and your heart begins to pound wildly. You have just found a $100 bill. What a lucky day!

Or suppose one lazy Saturday morning you are awakened by the ringing of the telephone. Sleepily you answer, "Hello?" Then you hear a voice telling you, "You are the lucky winner!" Wouldn't that make your day?

The exciting effect of good luck is that it makes you feel special, as if YOU have been chosen especially to receive this gift of luck. And to feel special makes you feel good, and that makes you a happy person.

But you can't rely on rare instances of big luck to make you feel special every day. You don't find money every day. And yet to feel so good would make such a difference in your life. What really counts, then, is to have a steady discovery of small instances of luck - lucklettes, you might call them.

How do you find lucklettes? Finding that $100 bill is almost like the flitting butterfly that came to you by pure chance. And yet there is more to it. You took that second look. Someone else may have dismissed the flutter as a piece of paper. And then you said, "I am lucky."   Someone else may have complained, "I could have used more."

Luck takes a positive attitude, and an appreciation of the good things that come your way. Some will call luck a blessing or good fortune. Others will say you have to be an optimist to have luck. But no matter what it is called, it is the person who recognizes his good fortune who will have luck. Take my father, for instance. When he turned sixty he said, "Yep, I'm a lucky man to be alive today, for life begins at sixty. Most of my enemies are dead, and the ones that remain are beginning to mellow."

Sometimes you have to look hard for a tiny ray of luck, that blessing. During the Second World War, Corrie ten Boom, author of *The Hiding Place*, was spending time in a concentration camp. She realized that without some hope, her life would be utterly miserable. Therefore, she prayed daily and thanked the Lord for the few good things she did have, including the fleas. She found that it was because of those fleas that the brutal sergeant rarely visited their barracks. Corrie ten Boom refused to give in to total defeat. She found something to be grateful for and called herself lucky. And that gave her hope.

I, too, have found luck all my life. My father once told me when I was a little girl, "Tine, you will always have luck." As one example he recalled how luck came to us during the Dutch Hunger Winter in 1945. People were starving and my family sat huddled at home, cold and very hungry. Then one day an airplane flew over and dropped food packages on our village. One such package fell in our street and as it hit the ground it burst open and sugar spilled from it. All the little children on our street, me included, ran outdoors, and we lay on our tummies licking up the sugar from the cobblestones. We were so fortunate. The package could have fallen somewhere else.

Ten years later we left our homeland. We came to America and the longer we lived here, the more we realized that we had come to the greatest country of all. I live here now blessed with wonderful parents, a loving family, dear friends, and great teachers. For all this I am   humbly grateful.

And when a day comes by when I am not so nice and not so grateful, my children help me through the gloom. One morning, five minutes before the school bus came, ten-year-old Michelle asked me, "Mama, have you seen my shoe?" My frustration mounted as I ran through the house, searching. Somewhat in amazement Michelle stood quietly on the side, watching her mother lose her cool. At last she said reassuringly, "Oh, Mama, don't worry. We'll find it when we move."

So you see that good luck is not like a butterfly which flits about and chances to settle upon one person's shoulder and not upon another's. Luck does not come from without, it comes from within. And unlike that butterfly which is difficult to catch, you can hold luck in your hands when you choose.

MICHAEL

Mike was his name. Michael. A big, good-looking Irishman, 32 years old. We met for lunch. An easy meeting. At times I casually propped my foot up on the wheel of his battery-operated wheelchair. Later he told me that had made him feel good because it meant that I felt comfortable in his space. "I am not abnormal," he said. "I am just as normal as anyone else, but you'd be surprised to know how many people ask me what I was like when I was still normal."

In a way I knew what he meant. Once I dressed up as a prostitute and for a joke met some friends for lunch at the Black Forest Inn. I had thought nothing of it because in my mind, in my image, I was still me, not how I appeared to others. My "me" was respectable, loving, intelligent, whole. The stares of people had startled and puzzled me. So I knew how he felt when he said he was normal, really.

We shared good ideas about his being a speaker and therefore a link between the "walkies" and the "crippies," as he referred to the "you" and "we."

With a strong yet gentle determination he is overcoming the hurt of not being like a "walkie," since his sport injury at age 15 left him a paraplegic and a wheelchair-user - NOT, he argued, confined to a wheelchair. That is confining and restricting.

He is trying to overcome the hurt of being considered so different, outwardly. He is trying to tell an awkward world that he belongs to them, an awkward world that feels shy and uncomfortable when confronted with something that is different from the norm. "Look inside my mind," he cries out. "I am not different."

He laughed easily and shared an inside joke with me, an outsider. "Hire a cripple, they're fun to watch." Not understanding the humor I cringed at his ability to see anything funny in that.

We talked openly, a man with a vision, and a need to reach people through the spoken word. "Look," he tells his audience, "if I can open a letter with my teeth and crippled hands, you, too, can overcome difficulties. But you have to

believe first that you can do it. Just believe it is possible."
He picked up a glass of water with his wrists and drank
from it.

Then we said goodbye. I leaned over and gave him a
hug. I saw a good-looking face, clear eyes, a ready smile, a
big Irishman. I walked to my car. He went in the opposite
direction. As I drove off he had already gone around the
corner. It was a sunny, beautiful spring day and as I
stopped at the intersection I looked down the street and saw
the back of a big, strong man in a wheelchair riding toward
his car. I looked at him for awhile, then sighed and
whispered to myself, "Oh, God." And drove on.

𝕀 was standing in the kitchen looking out the window and saw a robin. "Gee, he is beautiful," I thought to myself. What a pleasure he is to look at. And then I wondered if he ever felt he had no purpose in life. Do birds ever wonder about such things? But he gave pleasure by being so beautiful, and that could be his purpose, his gift in life.

He ran well and beautifully. Someone asked him why he ran. He answered, "Because that is my gift." Then I wondered, what is *my* gift in life? What is *your* gift? Do you know?

COFFEE BREAK

I sip my coffee and eat the chocolate éclair. What should I do now? Ask the waitress for another cup? I don't have to. She pours more of the black, bitter water. Three quarters full. Stingy, I think. As if reading my thoughts, she hesitates and then fills the last quarter to the rim. Delicious. I lift the cup and sip the hot steaming brew.

I look around. The man across the counter is fat, incredibly fat. How is it possible for a man to be so fat? He must have his clothes made specially for him. He cradles his cup of coffee, and it all but disappears in his hands. He gets up and labors as he awkwardly puts on his jacket. His stomach touches the back of his chair. He stumbles away and looks at me without seeing me.

The fellow next to me is a regular customer. I have seen him before in the same seat. He sighs continuously as he always sighs. He holds his lame right hand as he always holds it. He has finished his toast and coffee and newspaper. Then he takes his dentures out of his pocket, studies them, picks off a piece of lint. Quickly he looks around the room. No one is looking, and he shoves his false teeth in his mouth. He gets up and walks away the same way he does every time I see him, absorbed in thought.

To my left is a booth. Two couples sit there. Couples in their early sixties. I take a double look. The men are twins. Twins with twin twinkles in their eyes and twin laughs. They are having fun. Double fun.

AMERICA

I love America. Yet I am angry because I can't make that statement without fear of boring people, without fear of being ridiculed for saying something considered so mundane. Why should I not love this country that liberated my homeland, that fulfilled my parents' dream, that will be the country of my children?

What is happening to this country that I am so frequently discouraged from looking at the good and praising it? I have seen the good and lived it. Yet when I told some of my friends how I felt, they reacted with, "Oh, don't talk about such things. Look at all the bad things that are happening."

What is happening to this country that I should not be able to glow with pride and have pride returned when I tell a story that has been told a thousand times: the immigrant story. I do not live in ignorant bliss. I realize that our country faces gigantic problems. But these problems do not diminish my love for this country.

My parents were married in that tiny country by the North Sea, Holland. And they had dreams. Dreams to own a home, to travel, to be self-employed. But one day shock reverberated through our homeland. Holland was brutally sucked into World War II. The Hunger Winter came and my father and mother shared with their two young children a loaf of bread and a half-rotten cabbage. And because at times there was nothing else to eat, they ate tulip bulbs.

On May 5th, 1945, joyous bells began to peal. People filled the streets shouting with crazy happiness, "The war is over. Thank God for the Canadians and the Americans." From rubble and ashes Holland began to rebuild itself. But endless restrictions and red tape prevented my parents from building according to their dream.

My American aunt, visiting Holland, encouraged us, "Come to America. Everything is possible in America." And so in 1956 we came to this land of opportunity.

Immigrants my parents were. They packed their

belongings, said goodbye to all that was near and dear to them, and with boundless enthusiasm began to work and shape their dream. What was not possible in Holland then was possible in our new country. In a letter home my mother wrote, "We work hard, and soon we hope to buy our own washing machine. And we are getting spoiled. We eat ice cream almost every day."

My father got up at 4:30 in the morning and walked five miles to catch the train to work. Later someone gave him a bicycle, which was so clumsy that he could safely leave it leaning against the outside of the train station, unlocked. But he dreamed of a car, and when we bought our first one, a silver Chevy, we felt like royalty. The people in Holland envied us.

We worked hard, but laughed, too. I remember a kindly soul asking my mother one day, "Well, how are you doing?" She answered with what she thought was the appropriate expression for being very, very tired, "Ach, I feel like I am three sheets in the wind."

I get a lump in my throat when I see the flag of the United States being raised. That flag marched ahead of the troops which helped liberate my home country. That flag welcomed our family when my parents were in search of freedom to fulfill their dream.

I am the daughter of those immigrants. But I'm an American now, and I want to preserve that which I value and love. And if I don't love America, my children may not have an America. I fear the obvious lack of national pride, for without apparent love there may not be enough care, and without care, what future? Will my children eat tulip bulbs?

And who would liberate them?

It was bitter cold, and the sun shone upon the frozen ice. The snow was all gone. The contracting and expanding of that huge plate of lake ice sounded like some primitive music, as if the ice danced with the sun. It was a fantastic sound, continual, haunting, earthy, soulful.

Have you ever seen fear in the eyes of a bird? In the barn several sparrows had built their nests. These birds are fun to watch, but they do create an incredible mess with their droppings. One day the neighboring farmer stopped by, and he decided that the best way to get rid of them was to shoot them. He came back a few hours later with a friend and two BB guns. There was much excitement between the men, each bragging what good shots they were, how they had fought off dogs with knives, how they had killed a tom cat who was killing all the baby kittens, and what they would do in case of assault and burglary. And even though we had moved in and out of the barn all day long, I noticed a sudden silence which had not been there before. Did the birds sense death? "Just make sure they don't suffer," I said and stayed to make sure.

The farmer loaded his gun and aimed at a male sparrow sitting on one of the boards against the back wall, fifteen feet above the ground. Zzzapp, a pellet hit two inches below him in the wood. The bird crouched. Zzzapp went another pellet. It hit three inches above the bird. Zzzapp went another pellet. "You got his attention, anyhow," John, the friend, laughed. "Somebody's been goofing with the sighting," the farmer cursed.

I looked at the bird, and then I saw it. I felt it. The intensity of fear. The knowledge of being a target. The knowledge of being helpless in the face of attack. And suddenly it felt as if the pellets had hit deep in my heart. Childhood fears and fury arose within me. Tears came into my eyes. I moved to go out of the barn. "Why don't they just leave the birds alone, Mommy?" my child whimpered. I answered that I didn't know and then I went away.

I walked down to the creek and sat there for a long time. I noticed the multitude of flowers that grow in the wild. So many, many colors and varieties. And look, there on a stone close to the water, must be a hundred yellow butterflies, the small ones, the ones they say live only a short while. Someday I should make a photo album of all the beautiful things that live in the fields and woods.

Perhaps we fight with life, feeling that it has to be grabbed at just the right moment or it will pass us by. Perhaps we live in fear of a good life and approach it as something nearly unobtainable which we will miss unless we are at the right place at the right time. We want to control life, as if it is a commodity. Maybe this is all wrong. Maybe all that we search for, all the answers we seek, are there, if we would only stop controlling and fearing and fighting and instead make ourselves available and open to receive what we need and deserve.

Hope. It is a belief in the possibility of a solution, which has not presented itself as yet.

If we could know the past of the future,
We would not be so worried about the present.

Yesterday I went swimming at the YMCA. Afterwards I sat in the whirlpool for awhile. With me in the water were a young woman and a man. She was so excited because she was getting married. He asked her, "What is he like? Is he serious? I mean, is he serious about the future and things like that?"

"Oh, yea, he is really serious," she answered him enthusiastically. "Yea, he is really serious about the future and his job and about things like that. I am so happy. So excited. He is tall and has broad shoulders. He kind of gives the impression of being just another football player, but he really is not that at all. He really is nice. Last week we got our parents together. His parents are really interesting. They came from Poland, and they were in the concentration camp during the Second World War. You should hear them speak. Really interesting. So fascinating."

And with that she sank a little deeper into the pool, caressed by the hot, relaxing water.

So much innocence. Innocence about the past, innocence about the future. Oh, but why not? Let her enjoy the now, the romance. Let her enjoy what seems so wonderful, interesting, fascinating, exciting.

When I am worried about what others think of me, I really place the focus on them. If, however, I change the focus to me, on who I am and what I have to offer, then it will not matter what they think. Aha!

If you can just keep on thinking about something exciting that will happen tomorrow and the day after, always something exciting up ahead, no matter how insignificant, then nothing could really shatter you completely. In this light even death could be looked upon as exciting. You never know what will come after......(as long as it is not confronting you).

If I want happiness and riches I must be worthy of it.

Sometimes it is all right to allow yourself to be engulfed by the wind and the trees and take no notice of them. It is all right to become part of nature without appreciating it.

It's not the experience that is important, but how you are going to apply what you learned from it. Each of life's happenings prepare us for the next, but how well this preparation will serve us depends on how willing we are to learn and appreciate each step.

Hope in the future lies in
seeing the changing past.

FOR B.

After you experienced the frantic see-saw
Between hope and despair
And then the finality of her death,
You tried for awhile to attack life
With a forced and clutching grip.
You were going to live!
You were going to build things.
You were going to study.
You were going to work and travel.
You were going to renew life.
And you were going to live, live, live.....

And then one day,
These words became senseless,
Meaningless shouts.
You let go of the grip,
And you asked yourself,
Why?
Why should I work
And travel and study
And make things in an empty world?
Then you cried, not because of loss
But because of loneliness.
We friends stood around you
And reached out,
But could not touch you,
Because to be touched one has to be able to love.
You were unable yet to love.
We could only watch and wait.

Have you ever wondered why life is like the sea?
Why we stand upon the shoreline
To gaze forlorn in thought
At the endless rolling thunder
Of the waves.....
Why we hear it calling, calling
And our hearts yearn to hear it more?

Could it be the swells
That resemble our emotions?
Could it be the depth
Which holds answers never told?
Could it be a longing
For an answer in that vastness.....
Could it be the calling to which we run,
And then fear?

We sail ships upon its surface
In the rain and in the sun.
We frolic in the waves
And beg for them to take us
Farther out, or in...but always moving.
Yet when we let the sea surround us, gently
We begin to see a world that rolling waves had veiled.
It's calling, calling, calling
And our hearts yearn to hear it more.

AN AUTUMN RIDE

Easily I lifted the bicycle out of the car. I zipped my jacket shut, pulled on my gloves, and stood for a moment facing the forceful wind and gray, autumn sky.

No other sounds could be heard just then: the wind was taking care of that. No other people were there either. The loneliness felt good. Undisturbed I could participate in the aloofness nature somehow always holds over man. Strange. It's an aloofness, and yet a welcoming open arm you can hide in.

My golden lightweight bicycle felt so good as it took me through the prairie. The short grass shivered and tossed against the bellowing wind. My eyes stung. They teared. I had to close them momentarily.

I entered the forest. Puddles on the road reflected the sky's grayness. The tree trunks stood dark and heavy above the wet carpet of earthen-colored leaves. Reds were more red, yellows more yellow, oranges more orange, browns more brown. All of nature seemed more intense on this cloudy, chilly, damp day.

An owl protested my intrusion and flew laboriously away, while chickadees and sparrows playfully darted ahead of me. The quiet shelter, the resting wind, and then the sudden screaming of a bird as it took flight when I came too close.

I rode on. The path began to circle Hyland Lake which was rough and gray, waves pounding upon the dull foam-embroidered shoreline. A large flock of geese rested majestically on the water, facing the wind. Suddenly they took off. They flew squawking overhead. What in that haunting cry makes me want to follow? I want to do something. I am anxious. I feel rushed. But I must stand there, exposed and unprotected, surrounded by grasses and the wind. I see the giant birds leave, determined against the dark sky, and I, I am left behind, alone, small, seemingly insignificant.

29

I have gone now from that place in the prairie. I have other important things to do. But I can always go back again to that aloofness, to that welcoming open arm I can hide in. I can always again stand unprotected in the middle of that openness and let time pass quietly for a moment or two as I recall the cry of the geese, the strange sense of urgency, and yet the peace.

RACING

Yesterday I spent the day at the horse races with a friend. He took me around the Canterbury Downs for a six-hour introduction to horse racing. Running horses are a beautiful sight to behold. I got tears in my eyes every time they came across the finish line, and I don't know why. It has something to do with the all-out effort pulled from the jockey and his horse during those last few seconds. That is deeply thrilling for me, probably because I've been there myself; not in horse-racing, mind you, but in athletic racing. It is thrilling because for one vibrant, explosive, flirting moment a racer thinks that, with one last burst of energy, he can surpass all physical and mental limitations and soar, leaving others behind. When I sense that willingness of energy as it is being driven into and shared with a beast, something deep within me stirs.

And the gods smile because we will, after all, remain human. Only in our minds will we have wings. It is that attempt, however, to surpass limitations that afterwards makes us giggle and feel fulfilled. This joyful feeling is so intoxicating that we try again and again to bring about something supernatural; one more time we will go all out because perhaps this next time we'll fly and sing.

A TRAINING RIDE

 Saturday night. As I settle down to sleep I prepare myself for the training ride tomorrow morning. With this preparation I won't be tempted to stay in bed and sleep in. When I get up at 5:00 I'll simply follow the command of the evening before: "Ride 100 miles."

 Midweek I had bicycled 50 miles. Thursday I had put in a three-hour canoe session. Friday I ran for three hours. And to give my legs a rest, I swam only one hour on Saturday.

 At 4:55 my alarm goes off. I get up, dress, fill my water bottle, pack a banana and energy bar. By 5:15 I am on the road.

 There is a refreshing solitude in the summer, on an early Sunday morning. The sun is up. Everything looks rested. Nature is alive in all its glory while most of the city still sleeps.

 I feel sluggish, however. But with subservient obedience I follow last night's order: "ride 100 miles."

 After 15 miles I begin to feel better, loosening up and enjoying the countryside. The corn is knee-high and smells country-fresh. Wild flowers add gemlike surprises to the ditches and fields. A deer runs across the highway, and geese herd their gosslings off the road near a swamp.

 On these long rides I carry my double-size water bottle. Once in a while I take a drink, but am not really thirsty until near the 50-mile mark. I get off my bike for a few minutes. The sun is beginning to warm the air, and I stand in the shadow of a large, old oak tree, somewhere in Minnesota's farmland west of the Twin Cities. I eat my banana, part of the energy bar and drink water.

 By 65 miles I have emptied the water bottle. The inside of my mouth begins to feel dry, so I stop by a church to refill. The church bell has just finished ringing, and farmers in their Sunday best walk quietly through the main door. Self- conscious of my outlandish bicycling apparel and sweaty odor, I choose a side door. Two young boys, ignoring the solemnity of the holy ground, chase each other and giggle when they see me. They run past me out to the parking lot. Their father comes after them and with a stern reprimand whispers, "Get in there." I ask one man if he would be so kind as to fill up my water bottle. His friends seem embarrassed as he accepts my request and goes downstairs to the men's room to fill the bottle. I sense a sigh of relief when I ride on.

By 10:30 I reach my favorite little restaurant. I order water, coffee, orange juice, four pieces of toast, and four cookies--two chocolate chip and two oatmeal. Half an hour later I'm on my bicycle again, up the first long hill right outside the tiny town, and I become aware of the rising temperature. In the restaurant I'd heard on the radio that the high for today would be 98 degrees by noon. I believe it. Everything is beginning to heat up now - the air, the road, me. I douse myself with water once in a while and take a swig.

Seventeen more miles to go and I begin to feel sluggish again; tired, bored, heavy. I want to stop but can't because I promised my children I would take them out for lunch. So I ride on. An imaginary reporter is asking me, "How are you doing?" And I answer, "O.K." And he asks, "You think you'll make it?" And I answer, "Yes," with no enthusiasm, because I have none left. These conversations are also part of the training; I always get a positive response from myself, no matter how fatigued I get.

I ride on. Another curve. Another hill. When you are tired there seem to be so many up-hills and so few downs. I switch to automatic pilot; I can make it to the next farm house. Then, I can make it up the next hill, just concentrate on one small portion at a time, don't think of the long distance ahead.

My bottle is getting empty, and I am heating up. I have to decide. Should I pour the remainder on me or drink it? I don't want to stop for water. Perhaps I'll make it home.

Ten miles to go. I'm hot and thirsty, but I ride on. A brief shower momentarily cools me off, but not for long. It was so brief it only left dark spots on the road, like measles. Once more I lift the water bottle to my mouth. I suck on it, but it's dry. I ride on. Automatically my legs pump. I'm hung over the handle bar, staring straight ahead, watching the side of the road and the pot holes, otherwise mindless. Just get home.

Five miles to go and suddenly all I see is those rain drops on the road. They begin to irritate me. My eyes try to focus on them, but can't. I look further down the road in an effort to avoid the confusion below my wheels. But I only get more and more irritated at the disorientation those spots create before my eyes. In spite of the heat I feel chilled, and fury surprises me: those damn spots! Suddenly I realize I am in danger of being effected by hyperthermia. "Get off. NOW!" I command myself.

To my left is a gasoline station. I see a hose on the ground and with single-minded determination I turn on the water. To the utter amazement of the station attendant I drench myself, hair, back, front, arms. Then I drink and drink and drench some more. Some-one walks by and looks at me, and in that marvelous way that people have in restoring odd situations, he remarks, "Kinda hot, ain't it?"

"Yep," I reply.

I feel better now and am O.K. I ride home and hang up my bike. Another training session finished.

I was training for an athletic event. And yet that same sense of awareness of a goal, the self-coaching, self-awareness of progress and deliberate switching to automatic pilot, one small step at a time when continuing appeared so difficult, are directly applicable to daily life when situations become seemingly unsurmountable. And thus, the training ride became another lesson in life.

𝕴 have completed the 500-mile Minnesota Border-to-Border Triathlon now, the first woman in its history to solo against two-person relay teams. It is a four-day event, covering 400 miles of bicycling in the first two days, 50 miles of running the third day and 50 miles of canoeing on the fourth day. Five hundred miles through Minnesota's farm-land and over her waterways from the border of Iowa, north to the border of Canada.

On Wednesday afternoon, my father, our newly-married friends, Jim and Janet, and I drove in two vehicles from Minneapolis to Luvern on the Iowa border. The four of us slept in a tiny motel room with Janet and me in a twin bed that sagged in the middle. My Dad slept on a rickety camping cot brought from home, and Jim was on the floor with his long torso taking up every available left-over floor space.

That night I tried every trick in the book to relax. But even though I did not feel particularly excited or eager with anticipation, one part of my mind must have been very busy because I just would not fall asleep. I probably slept an accumulated two hours. The next morning, however, I could not worry about that. I had a thirteen-hour day ahead of me, bicycling 200 miles north to St. Cloud.

We got up at five, dressed, ate something from the food bag and drank some juice. At ten minutes to six we lined up at the starting line - a yellow spray-painted squiggly line on the highway outside the sleepy little town. Every once in a while a car would slow down and inch through the non-challant, peculiar-looking bunch of cyclers in their full racing regalia. There were 24 teams. The Mayor made a short speech and then sent us off with a gun shot at 6:00. By this time people had found out that I was the only woman doing the race solo and I received a great deal of encouragement, oh's and ah's and this continued throughout the race. It was a good, friendly feeling. One newspaper reporter asked me why I was doing this. "Gosh," I laughed, "I don't know."

Jim and Janet took turns off and on riding with me.

Their support and help was beautiful and invaluable and resulted in a very close friendship. One of the things a long-distance athlete has to contend with is boredom. Oh, it can get mighty boring. So you ride with your feet at an angle to the left, and then to the right, and then both pointing inwards to the count of 25. I sang songs, "100 bottles of beer on the wall," "99 bottles of beer on the wall," and then argued with myself whether I was at 76 or 75 bottles. Then I switched to Mozart arias and piano concertos. I smiled at the cows and said "Hi," admired the yellow flowers in the ditches, and counted off the miles, backwards from 200.

The times I had company on the road were supportive and very much needed. Yet there were other times when I needed to be alone with the surrounding silence to which a long distance athlete grows accustomed. Times when you become aware of the fact that ultimately it is totally up to you to keep on going with whatever mental tenacity you can muster up. It's an awe-inspiring feeling and delicious, because no boss, no client, no one can take this control over your own success away from you.

The event may well be called, "Why I ate my way across Minnesota." Every couple of hours my Dad fixed food and vitamins for me and told me to eat, whether I felt like it or not. Nourishing intake is very important on multi-day physical endurance feats. He did a super job fixing Shaklee soups and other dishes on the camping stove in the van, although at times the stuff was burnt and the whole wheat bread had become soggy. It never did dry out no matter how carefully we laid it on the warm motor covering, turning it over every once in a while in the hope of creating something which might be called "toast."

I covered 195 miles on the bicycle the first day and about 215 on the second day to Virginia, Minnesota. The second day we had a head wind even stronger than the first day, and at times I couldn't resist a frustrated scream. During training at home you know that even on the windiest day, you will always have a tail wind some part of the ride. When I realized that I would fight a continual, unsympathetic northerly blast, I had to concentrate to overcome the dicouraging feeling of endlessness. But somehow you continue and peddle on and on and on, counting off the miles one by one.

Besides the 10- to 15- minute breaks to eat, I was in the saddle 13-1/2 hours the first day and 14-1/2 the second. Toward the middle of the second day my potty stops became longer and longer and my crew had to chide me and urge me on. At one stop I found myself in a rather embarrassing predicament. After relieving myself on my hounces, I tried to stand up, but found that my thighs had tightened. I could not get up. So I sat, mooning the ants of the North woods, unable to move. Slowly I let myself down on all fours and, with my bare bottom facing due south, I crawled to a nearby tree, hoisted myself up and at last resumed my proper biking attire. It was a good, private laugh for me and the shameless northern fields.

That evening I requested four baked potatoes. I was craving them. Unfortunately two were bad, and since we had brought them to our motel room there was nothing to do but go back to eating more soggy bread and peanut butter.

The third day was the most difficult day. I had averaged five to six hours sleep at night and I had never run 50 miles before. A marathon had been my longest running feat thus far. The first 25 miles went by surprisingly fast. Janet ran with me, chatting, joking. We were having a good time. We passed a man working in his garden and he asked us where we were headed. "Cook," we called out. "Cook?" he exploded incredulously. "Fifty miles from here? Yea, you're cooks alright," and shaking his head he disgustingly pulled out more weeds. The laugh was good for at least three miles.

Then it became progressively more difficult. I walked up every hill and ran the downs and flats till the last twelve miles. Was it ever going to end? I was forced to walk short bits more frequently. But it was a Catch 22 situation. I was so fatigued I could hardly run, walking at first felt good. But it stiffened me up so much that the first minute of running was agony. One step at a time. Go ahead and hurt. It is in my body, not my head. I'm separate from the pain. It

37

will not last. And next to me was Jim. How was he doing? OK. Hang in there. You will make it. Janet was driving the car next to us, playing the music from *Chariots Of Fire*. It was her turn to rest. Behind me was Dad in the van, with the banner SUPPORT CREW MINNESOTA BORDER TO BORDER RACE. All supporting me because I wanted to achieve a personal goal. Incredible!

I drank a lot of fluids, often forcing them down because nothing tasted good anymore. Every mile I ate a tiny bit of food, one grape, spitting out the pulp, one slice of orange, again spitting out the pulp because the roughage made me nauseated. One calcium, one tablet vitamin C, one B. Amazingly, as much as my body was being punished, my spirits stayed high and positive throughout the entire four days, even by the end of the run when I was hurting more than I had ever experienced.

Nothing takes the place of endurance training, but I feel that my success was made all the more possible because of the excellent nutrition program and mental training which I had followed throughout my preparatory months. Daily I had visualized seeing myself crossing the finish line, being congratulated and being written up in the newspaper. It was this automatic visualization which had also helped me survive and continue training twice through a two-week period when I lost all hope and believability in being able to complete the race. I faked believing until I began to believe again. It worked.

About seven miles from the end of the run some of my other friends, who had already finished, came to meet me. They took pictures, encouraged me on, praised me, and told me it was alright to cry, which I did when the beauty of their human compassion and support, their total devotion to seeing me finish got the best of me.

I turned within myself - alone with my pain, alone with my goal, alone with my me, and yet was unselfishly supported by my friends. It resulted in an increased awareness of the power and beauty of relationships and friendships which ordinary bustling life so often overlooks.

The fourth day we got up at 4:15 a.m. to drive 45 minutes

to Vermillion Lake, where the 50-mile canoe section began. It was misty and must have been a beautiful sight for those standing on shore to see 26 canoes slipping off into the mists of dawn. We got lost and it cost us at least half an hour before we found the dam and the beginning of the Vermillion River.

Now I must explain that there was one other person who was doing the race solo, an American from Hawaii. In the beginning people paid equal amount of attention to him. However, it soon became evident that he was an extremely disagreeable fellow, argumentative, boisterous. He called himself Fabulous Eddy. But because I passed him up every day, he soon became known as Fast Eddy.

Picture yourself now a group of five canoes, paddling close together across a huge lake in the fog. We saw no shore line. Fast Eddy was with us, but as will happen with a solo canoe, the wind caught his stern and gently spun him around so that he was slowly disappearing off to our right. He was obviously not an experienced canoeist. One person called out to him, "Here, Eddy. This way." Where upon another joker said, "Oh, let him go. That's the way I would like to remember him, disappearing in the mist." I laughed so hard that I worried, lest the water god take revenge on my cruelty and make me tip. About 15 minutes later we looked to our left and there, as the mists parted, we saw a solo canoe with Eddy, sitting statue still. Was it Eddy's ghost? And then he disappeared again, not to be seen or heard of till 11:00 that night. Little more is known about him except that he brought back a broken paddle, a scratched-up canoe, and was madder than a wet hen.

The canoe section was equally beautiful to the rest of the event. Once we crossed the lake and entered the river, the mists evaporated and the sun came out. I was in a solo canoe and Jim and Janet were in my C2 canoe. For the first 24 miles things went well, except that Janet became more and more tired. She had done extremely well all three days but both she and Jim had underestimated 50 miles of canoeing. After six hours we came to the first bridge where my Dad gave us more peanut butter and jelly sandwiches.

Shortly afterwards I realized that Janet was burnt out. I had to make a decision as to how we could continue without losing too much time. We could not be out on the river in the dark and for the next 24 miles there were no drop-off points. The water was low that year and we continually had to be on the look-out for rocks.

I proposed that we put Janet in my solo canoe, tow her, while Jim and I paddled the rest of the way in the C2. Later she told me how terribly humiliating this had been for her. She felt she had let me down. But I never knew, and her constant joking, combined with my fatigue, caused me to have spells of hilarious laughter. It all made the miles slip by, around another curve, across another portage, of which there were 13 in all. It was hard work for the next 7-1/2 hours, towing Janet- especially since Jim, although very strong, was not skilled enough to prevent the canoe from being pulled sideways by the wind and current and tow. This meant that I continually had to correct our course- a doubling demand on my output.

At the finish line I received a warm welcome and was honored with a special voyageur's initiation. In the olden days the young men of the Northwoods who made their first solo run down the river to the Canadian border were donned at the end with a hat and sash amidst plenty of merrimaking and drinking. So I, too, was given the colorful woolen hat and sash for around my middle. While taking a swig of "shrub," a beverage originally made from fermented local berries but now substituted with Southern Comfort, I was liberally sprinkled with a cedar bough dipped in the cool, lake water. I was blessed with the voyaguer's initiation rites, since I had soloed my first run down the river. It was most festive.

And then it was all over. My mental training had paid off well. I never hesitated or wondered if I was going to make it. I just did it using all the skills that winners in all walks of life use: a clearly-defined goal, visualization, automatic pilot, humor, relying on the support of friends.

When I came home there were lots of flowers, the flag hung out, posters of Welcome greeted me, and hugs and tears and "Mama, we knew you could do it." I received a winner's homecoming. I was 43 years old, recently separated, going through divorce. I was facing financial panic, in the process of setting up my own business, and raising two teenagers. However, at that moment I felt like a winner.

Yes, I did it. But when someone a few days later asked me how I felt about my accomplishment, I stared off into space, shrugged my shoulders and could only answer, "Well, it's just one of those things I did."

Perhaps the reality of it all will hit me later. But life goes on. When I drive around the city through the hurried traffic, I think back to those lonely Minnesota highways and country ways which I traveled on my own power - 500 miles of it. When I take out the map of Minnesota and see what I covered, I shake my head in disbelief at what the human body is capable of. It took me months of intense training, built on a base of seven years of endurance athletics. But what about those loons who cried somewhere in the mists of Lake Vermillion? In a few more weeks they will start heading south and without any training cover thousands of miles. How do they do it? And why? Instinct drives them to seek warmer climates. But what about us? We don't need to put ourselves through such physically-demanding endurance to survive. So why do we do it? For glory? For something called self-satisfaction, fulfillment? They seem common, overused words. And yet when you have experienced pushing yourself to the limit and still had more left, and you shared that with someone else, you realize you experienced getting a glimpse of something which makes us more than what we think we are. We are then filled with a quiet, exciting knowledge of, yes, there is more to life than everyday concerns. There is more to friendship than a "Hi, how are you?" There is more ability in each of us than we are usually aware of. This race was my final big athletic event. It was, however, the beginning of a new understanding of the enormous strengths and potential in all of us.

A WINTER MARATHON

$\mathfrak{N}$ow I have run a winter marathon. It went well, although during the last five miles my legs had an increasing argument about which one was going to quit first, with or without my permission. But I won out, in spite of their lack of total understanding support, and I crossed the finish line with a personal victory. Why did I run a winter marathon? Why not?

An hour before the race: I stand in a long line waiting to get my race packet which contains my race number. We are inside the small local airport. A particular pre-race sweaty odor permeates the air. People mingle, shouting, talking, laughing. Suddenly I hear over the loudspeaker that those who are running the entire distance may get their packets at table four. Relieved I leave the long line of half marathoners and walk over to table four. "Thevenin," I say to the lady, "starts with a Th." I get my packet and, glancing over to the long line, see Keith, my friend. "Hey," I yell, "What are you doing over there? Aren't you running the whole thing?" "Nah," he answers, "what for? I've got nothing to prove." "Chicken," I tease in order to support my own justification for running a marathon in sub-zero weather. I move to the women's changing area to put on the last touches of running gear; an extra lightweight sweater, windbreaker and woolen hat. I wait in the long line for the last toilet call. Gosh, women take a long time.

Ten minutes before the race we all line up outside. Nervous giggles. "What am I doing out here?" someone whines as if expecting a sane answer. People look at him as if he has lost his mind. You learn to ignore folks like that. Over the PA system we are told that at the thirteen-mile mark Red Cross volunteers will help the full marathon runners turn around. (The course is out and back.) I burst out laughing at the mental picture of seeing runners plodding along, plodding, plodding into the frigid wind, thrusting, aching, until suddenly someone grabs them by the shoulders, spins them around, half a turn and with a shove sends them back, plodding, plodding, plodding into the frigid wind, thrusting, aching.....indeed, what for?

One minute to go. We stand ready, packed like sardines on the road, shielding each other from the biting wind. "Wait," a voice rises above the din, "I have to go to the bathroom." Laughter. Then, suddenly, the gun goes off. A roar lets loose. Twenty-six miles lie ahead. After one mile somone asks, "Are we having fun?" "Yea," somebody answers with doubt in his self-assuring voice, "I am having fun."

Slowly the tight, colorful bouncing crowd begins to stretch out, the front runners setting a pace, carefully weighing the benefits of drafting and passing. Most runners, however, do not run for fierce competition, but to do their personal best, and thus accept their position in the pack. At the 6-1/2 mile mark the half-marathoners turn around, while once in a while a runner peels off as if thrown into space. For a minute my reasoning tries to convince me that I, too, could turn around back to where it is warm with laughter and good cheer. But no, I spin off and suddenly find myself a lonely runner. "Good luck," someone shouts. She had been running behind me and was on her way back home. "Thanks," I wave. "See you in a couple of hours."

Police direct the traffic at intersections. Every three miles there is a water stop with smiles and encouraging words, all volunteers who give hours and support to us few who want to run twenty-six miles on a very cold, January day. To prove what?

At fifteen miles my legs begin to hurt. I judge. Is this a hurt that may cause long-term injury or just lactic acid filling my muscles? Continually now, I am judging, weighing, questioning, changing my gait, trying to hang loose, feeling the growing pain, wondering whether I'll make it to the end, yet focusing on crossing the Finish line.

Then one mile to go. It's the longest mile. My thighs are burning with pain. I'm chilled. The wind, cold and unforgiving blasts across the open field. My woolen cap is pulled low over my head. The collar of my sweater is up over my numb chin. I put on the extra pair of wool mittens I carried along.

Step after step I am running, slowly bucking the winter wind. My eyes sting. Occasionally I look up hoping to see signs of the Finish banner. All I am aware of now is the intense burning pain in my legs and my thirst. I am so very thirsty. How can I go on? "Why not walk?" a voice enticingly beckons.

"No," I answer, "I will run."

And then suddenly it is over. The actual crossing takes but a split second. It is, after all, just a thin white line on the frozen ground. Someone takes my registration number to be fed into the computer with my time. He studies my face and asks me how I feel. Do I need help? "No, thank you. I am fine. Just very thirsty." He is kind. Everyone is so kind, so supportive. Somewhat in a daze I walk inside where it is warm, and I drink water, tea, beer and know that I have accomplished what I set out to do.

Indeed I wanted to run a winter marathon to see if I could cover that distance. Yet, I discovered more on that run. I experienced again that very special kindness, support, and those smiles from strangers who wanted me to succeed on my journey. Again I am left with a wonderful feeling of accomplishment which, however, cannot be explained, only experienced. And that is really why it is rather senseless to try to explain, "why." No one has yet been able to do that. So the unknowing will continue to shrug their shoulders in disbelief and ask, "why?" The knowing will continue to shrug their shoulders with belief, but an inability to put into words, "Why not?"

℔ once had my ear frostbitten. The time was 2:30 in the afternoon. The temperature had reached its high for the day, minus nine degrees, with a wind chill of.....can't remember, but it was awful. After skiing for half an hour, I came back into the warming house. Involuntarily I touched my right ear, but what I felt was not my ear but a piece of wood. Wood???? "Hey," I yelled out in surprise, "part of my ear is frozen." My ear became an instant object of great curiosity. The ski patrol, a handsome, tall young chap (of course), readily available (naturally), came rushing onto the scene (pronto vivace). He gingerly lifted my long hair and exclaimed, "Hey, fellows, come over here. This is a fine example!"

Yes, Mom, I know you told me to always wear a good hat.

WINTER OF MY ADDICTION TO CROSS-COUNTRY SKIING

In the winter of 1978 I became addicted to cross-country skiing. I plunged into it with the zeal of one newly converted. No more was " blue" the innocent wax for all snow conditions. Instead, waxing became a subject hesitantly discussed with "real skiers," and bravely promoted to beginners. The old comfortable pair of winter slacks was hidden away; knickers and long socks were donned as the only way to go. Even the once-civilized handkerchief took a back pocket. Occasional "snotcicles" became acceptable facial adornments.

If I skied less than 10K at a time, I felt I had done a great disservice to the cause. And when someone casually handed me my first race registration form, I thought Mecca had come to town. I ran to the mail box with form and check exhuberantly stuffed in a snow white envelope. How great I felt!

And I have felt great ever since about this invigorating sport. But I must admit that one day as I was being transported to yet another race, a reflective mood settled over me, and I couldn't help but muse with a friend how incredible it actually was that somehow I found myself among thousands of people who had been lured into this mad activity. Let's take a closer look at those races for instance. Just think. In the bleak early morning hours, stark school buses take hordes of skiers to a starting line. (This after a restless night, the effect of having eaten too much pre-race pasta and being filled with nervous anticipation.)

Most people accept the ride patiently while being shaken and jossled by the hard benches of the vehicles. Mittened hands clutch skis and poles for reassurance of the reality of the situation. Participants yawn or talk or doze, but all assume to be looking forward to that grueling experience of pushing their bodies beyond their daily limits. To make the experience more bearable, the skiers wear colorful hats and shapely outfits, and as bait, a little medal dangles in the air many kilometers down the trail.

46

And all for what reason? Let me tell you mine. It's the beaming faces, the sore knees, the tingling feeling all over. It's the excitement and the comradeship of the participants. It's that elated, wonderful feeling of having accomplished a goal. What a great sport!

The other day a friend and I were skiing along the tracks at a fast pace, making good time and thoroughly enjoying the winter sport, when we approached an older couple who were shuffling along. When they saw us coming they moved off the track and watched us in amazement. The gentleman couldn't resist commenting, however, "Why so fast? Why such a hurry? What are you running away from?"

Ah, yes, the young and restless, the retired and peaceful!

Even in practice don't quit short of your goal, for in a real race, they won't move up the finish line.

The blizzard has spent itself. While yesterday the trees squeaked and cracked when howling winds tore through the branches and twigs, today they stand motionless against an ashen sky. All was quiet when I awakened this morning and looked outside. A rabbit had made fresh tracks over the new white carpet. The snowman's hat lay half buried where the wind had tossed it, and only the top of the red scarf was visible from around the snowman's neck.

America is like a quilt. Patches of land held together with stitchery of barbed wire.

ℒ work with lists. Every day I make a list of things to do. Today's list read, "Call home." A scribble. A reminder to call my mother and father. Call home. Home. Decorah, Iowa, is not my home town. I did not grow up there. My parents moved there a few years ago. Yet the house where my parents live, no matter where that is, is home.

Sometimes, as I lie down at night the idea of sleep feels so good I wish I could stay awake to enjoy it.

The fun thing about dieting is that you can always start tomorrow!

It is amazing how easily we forget hours of fun and joy and peace when we are engaged in a raging battle which may last only fifteen minutes.

RACHEL

Emergency Room, Methodist Hospital, 12:30 a.m. early December. Lying on an examination table to have my hand sewn up, I at last began to tremble. "Well," the surgeon asked, "tell me what happened."

Since the first three inches of a predicted ten inches of snow had already fallen, I decided, as I put my two German Shepherd dogs out in the back yard, that I would shovel the driveway. The snow was coming down gently but steadily, and I shoveled. It is peaceful when snow is falling late in the evening. Suddenly I heard piercing yelping. I ran to the back and with horror saw Lobo, the male, standing over Rachel with his head at her throat. I called out sharply, "Lobo!" but he did not move. Then I realized what horrible thing had taken place. While playfully biting the back of Rachel's neck, Lobo's lower canine teeth had hooked around her narrow nylon collar and in struggling to free himself, he was cutting off her air. Her collar became a tourniquet.

I rushed over. Nothing but a few panic-stricken grunts escaped Rachel's air passage. She was being strangled to death. Although I was thinking clearly, I was frantic. I tried to locate the clasp, but could not find it. It was too deeply drawn into her fur and skin as Lobo pulled and twisted to free himself. My fingers got caught between her teeth. I yanked and quickly examined my hands. I found deep lacerations. The struggle continued. Meanwhile time was clicking by, and with a clear, surreal, detached perception I saw gentle, fluffy snow falling on three struggling figures. I was bewildered by the fragility and brevity of life, and yet awed by the power with which life will resist death.

I knew of but one solution. I left the writhing dogs, ran inside, down the stairs to get my scissors. How long had I been gone? Too long? I knelt beside the dogs. Rachel twisted her head once more and looked at me with frightened, helpless eyes and then passed out. I cut twice without getting any resistance. Do what you must, I thought frantically: repair the damage later. You MUST cut the collar. So I dug deeply at the back of her neck, clear of her throat. I felt resistance. I bore down with all my strength. The collar fell off, freeing Lobo and allowing air to rush into Rachel's lungs.

She lay still for a moment and then got up, wobbling. Both dogs looked at me dazed. I extended my hand and said "Rachel?" My voice cracked. She slowly wagged her tail and came over to lick my face. Lobo only smiled. He rarely kisses.

The snow was still coming down, like time, patiently going on. It was so very quiet and still. There I sat, on the ground with two stunned German Shepherd dogs--blood on my hands, blood on the snow, blood on the white wooden gate. And suppose I had not recognized in time what was happening? Rachel would be dead. Oh, no!

When someone you value or love dies, all you can do is carry on their tradition. And that is a beautiful thought because it gives one purpose, a continuance, a look forward into the future.

Whenever I am confronted with a question concerning health, the environment, childrearing, I ask myself, "How had nature intended for it to be?" I try to find that example and then see how far removed we have become. And then I try to understand how we can live in our 20th century and still have respect for and live in harmony with nature.

Run with me children
Through this dale
Up to yonder tree.
I'll throw you daisies in a chain
If you'll throw them back to me.
Let's laugh and shout and love and be,
Catch it, catch it, catch it!

And I quote Michelle with the wisdom of a four-year-old: "Please wait. When you go too far ahead of me, I get the feeling that I have farther to go!"

"Mama, why are you always awake at night when I need you? All I have to say is 'Mama' and you answer me. It's almost as if you stay awake all night"--Michelle, five years old.

"That's the way Mamas are," I answer.

Children are too young to deny childhood and approach life with the maturity of an adult. But how many of us realize that fully?

We went sledding by the school, my children and I. And as we trudged up the big hill, Michelle slipped. As she struggled to get up, I caught her and gave her my hand. Automatically she eased her hand into mine, and I helped her up the rest of the way.

The significance of being a good parent then occurred to me. Children rarely appreciate this ambition. My reward as a parent will come when my children have children of their own and parent them as I have reared mine. Through our children we are really rearing our grandchildren.

A child does not think and then act negatively. He responds to a feeling deep inside. For us to overcome being personally affected by negative reactions is a major accomplishment in maturing.

The purpose of parental wisdom is not to give it to our children when we are ready, but when they are ready. It is therefore imperative that we are with our children during their formative years.

During my childrearing years, I have developed faith in my children: their honesty, their ability to handle life, their feelings of responsibility. It is not what I see in my children, however, that is so important, but what I feel deep within; a trust in them.

STAY WITH ME

My twelve-year-old daughter, Yvonne, was sitting in the dentist's chair in a dental surgeon's office. She was to have two upper bicuspids extracted, the first major step in her orthodontal program. She was anxious and apprehensive of the strange surroundings and great unknown. I kissed her forehead and asked, "Afraid?" She nodded and smiled. I understood.

Yvonne had asked me to stay with her until she "went to sleep." I readily agreed, for I do not believe in leaving anyone who requests emotional support. And so, with a bit of frustration on the nurse's part, I was allowed to remain in the room while preliminary steps were taken: blood pressure and pulse. Shortly after that the surgeon strutted in and told me I could now leave and wait in the reception room. Yvonne took hold of my arm and said quietly, "I want you to stay here."

The tension in the room intensified. "We don't allow that," the doctor informed us, standing against the wall, arms folded in front of him. Realizing the heat of the conflict, I asked the doctor if I could speak with him in the hallway. Once out of the room he told me that my daughter's request was totally uncalled, for since the operation was entirely routine. I should not question his method. After all, he had been in practice for over fifteen years. I responded that it may be routine for him, but it was not routine for Yvonne and that I could certainly be given credit for knowing my daughter, since I had lived with her for twelve years. He would not bend, however. Under no circumstances would I be allowed to remain in the room because, for one, it was too small!

After more fruitless discussion, I decided to speak with Yvonne and let her have the final decision. "Doctor," I said, "I feel we are getting no understanding from you." He retorted, "I don't think I would ever be able to give you the type of understanding you require." I looked at him briefly and before walking away responded, "I think you are entirely correct." I went to Yvonne and told her I could not remain in the room, upon which she got up from the dental chair and said, "Then we are not staying." In the elevator she cried, "Why doesn't he understand me?"

What type of psychology would support this suggested violation of trust? For twelve years I nurtured a trust between Yvonne and me. The doctor had tried to urge me, "Just let me go in there now and do the job. The longer we stand out here the more she will think we are plotting some kind of scheme." No, dear doctor. Yvonne trusts me. I have never intentionally violated this trust. She knows I will give her the support she needs, when she needs it. No more and no less.

I searched and found an agreeable doctor who was kind and gentle. The last thing Yvonne remembers before "going under" was my reassuring touch and the understanding nurse telling her how great she was doing, which gave her the confidence that everything was going fine. We can all handle a great deal of stress when we have the emotional support of a loved one.

What is the hurry of forcing a twelve-year-old to handle fear by herself? What are we afraid of? That she will never learn to handle fear? Yet more trust and security will develop from giving support and understanding than from withholding it, for true feelings of security cannot be forced upon someone. Only the right conditions allow it to develop. And just suppose Yvonne would always, for the rest of her life, want someone to be there when she visits a doctor. What is wrong with that? Really? Isn't there something wholesome and all right to be able to admit, "I need you?"

A friend told me that once she had taken an elderly neighbor lady to the doctor for the removal of a wart. She parked the car and helped the lady into the office. Just as she was ready to leave, her friend looked at her with imploring eyes and begged, "You are going to stay with me, aren't you?"

Need does not choose one age above another. A sign in an African Children's Hospital reads: "Please hear my cry,

69

even if you do not understand."

You fall in love and you marry. And then comes the time of discovering who your spouse is, who you are. Discoveries laced with pleasures, disappointments, agonies, surprises, joys.

When you hold two magnets close together the right way, they will attract one another. If you hold them the wrong way, you feel a strong, unpleasant resistance. They are pushing each other away. Relationships can be that way.

I felt rejected: therefore he said I needed counseling.
He felt nothing, so he was perfect.

The perch of perfection is a desolate place.

He thought he could play God and peek into another's mind. He read her diary without permission. What he found instead was the evil of his own image staring him in the face. And this evil became part of him, not God.

All negotiations ought to take place on top of a hill, so that the persons can remain in contact with the wide, endless expanse of the universe, making their problems small by comparison; real, but nevertheless small.......by comparison.

Don't hang on too tightly to one moment of life because life is stronger than you, and unless you flow with it, it will eventually break you. That is a poetic way of saying it is OK to hate and scream and cry once in a while. It's just that some of us do it more freely than others, while others have forgotten what it feels like.

My divorce is final. I feel as if a storm has passed and a calm has settled. I have closed a door behind me and I am looking onto a wide, open field. It is sunny.

I am not a victim of divorce, but an active participant in one of life's greatest tragedies.

ℐ had lunch with Wayne. One of his past renters joined us for a short while. She was young, unmarried, a legal secretary. During our conversation she told us she really enjoys working with divorce cases. "They are so interesting," she admitted. "You really get to know those people. You talk with them every day. Many times they just want someone to listen to them. Although that sometimes really gets to be a bother. But in general I love to do divorce cases. And I am always sorry when they are over with because then you lose contact with the people. There is always so much involved with those cases. You wouldn't believe it."

Well, then she had to rush off because she had to record yet that day how many times and for how long each client had called and talked so they could be billed correctly. Goodbye. And then she ran off to her divorce cases like the secretary of some club. Club? Yes, miserable, yes. A club which demands pain for initiation. Pain of which she knows nothing. Yet she is their secretary.

The amazing thing about an "ex" of a divorce is that you never find yourself actually speaking to the terrible, horrible, awful ex. Wonder where they are hiding?

With great concern people tell me, "Why don't you get married again!" Then I answer, "Good idea, but every time I go to the store, they are out."

After my divorce I had taken life and looked at it squarely and said, with a no-questions-asked attitude, "I want no love for awhile. I need to heal." And then Jim showed kindness and interest, a comrade in thought and expressions and insights. He might as well have written my poems, my pieces. He hugged me for just a moment, and I felt strength and assurance which matched the feelings and relationship he has with his mountains. It did not stir emotions of love in me. I just like him. Yet, I felt a crack, a perplexing spiderweb crack in what had seemed a successful, impenetrable shield. And for some strange, irritating reason I have felt so depressed, so close to tears.

FOR YVONNE AND MICHELLE

Yesterday I walked through the woods, and it was beautiful. The sun was shining, the birds were singing and the flowers were blooming. It all felt so good and right. I loved those woods.

Not that my walks had always been perfect. I had been there and been drenched by a sudden, unexpected shower. I had been there in the freezing cold when all of summer's beauty seemed lost, and I wondered if it would ever return, if I would ever walk among the flowers again and hear the birds sing and feel the soft, comfortable ground beneath my bare feet.

It did. It all came back. And the bitter cold and lonesome woods made me appreciate the loveliness of summer. It made me understand what it meant to be cold and lonesome. Remembering those feelings, I realized that those woods were more than beauty. Having experienced those woods in winter as well as summer made me glad, because it reassured me that one season inevitably leads into another...always changing.

That was yesterday. Or so it seems, but it was long ago. Yet I still remember taking that lovely walk. And then the next day it was all gone. Just gone. Nothing was left. No trees, no birds, no flowers. And the soft ground was black with ashes.

I remember the shock I felt at seeing smoke and fire destroying that forest. My beautiful woods. I saw deer running and raccoons, and I wanted to go in and rescue the animals that could not escape. Many of them made it, but some died in the fire that raged through those woods. My beautiful woods.

After the shock I tried to pretend it was all a bad dream. For awhile I convinced myself the fire had not destroyed my woods. "Tomorrow," I promised myself. "Tomorrow you will be walking there again, and you will know it was all a bad dream."

84

But tomorrow came, and I saw that my woods were still black and burned, their beauty gone, and I wept. How would I ever feel good again? How would I ever glimpse the deer again? Everything was gone, burned up. It would take forever to grow a new forest, and where would I be all that time with nowhere to go, no place to walk and sit and feel good and right?

I felt so lonely and empty. Why had my lovely woods burned? Why had it happened to me? Why?

And then I became angry. I kicked the ashes, and my feet got black, and I didn't care. I picked up a rock and threw it against a tree stump. It crumbled, and I didn't care. I screamed out at the forest that wasn't there anymore, "I hate you," and I didn't care because it couldn't hear me anyway, and I felt more burned and hurt than the forest and screaming made me feel good.

And then I felt confused because I cared deeply and perhaps I could have prevented the fire.

And then I wept some more because I was so angry and felt so hateful and awful and sad and lonely. I wanted to make that forest whole again, but couldn't . This was not winter when things only seemed to be gone. Then you knew everything was just hiding, sleeping through the cold months. And although you couldn't see or feel the leaves and flowers, you just knew that in a little while all would come out again. But this time it was different because it had been burned up, destroyed, never to come back.

Or so it seemed.

Time passed and one day, out of habit I walked to the place where the woods had been. Looking across a hillside I saw delicate new green grass, like a gentle breath, sweeping the ground, and a startled bird suddenly took flight a little distance ahead of me.

That also seems like yesterday. And now I am sitting on a rock in the woods, my lovely new woods. Small trees surround me, and a bunch of flowers are lying next to me. I'll take those home.

While I am sitting here I catch a glimpse of a deer. He looks at me for a long time. Scars of the fire are still all around me. Some of the bigger tree stumps will be there for a long time. When I see them I feel a little like crying all over again, because they remind me of the forest I used to walk in.

And that is how it feels when something whole and good and dear to you is destroyed. One day you wake up and that beautiful thing is gone. You feel lonely, sad, angry, and wonder how everything could ever be right again. But somehow they are. Things turn out right again. The fire did not take the woods away forever; it just seemed that way. Some things from the early woods are gone, and I miss them. Yet other things are in my woods now which I had never seen before.

And the deer came back, after all, and so did the flowers. Here, have some.

How innocent were my younger years. They were not even hopeful. They were years in which I simply expected nothing else but goodness, in which I had high ideals, so high that I ignorantly, deliciously criticized those who did not conform to my high ideals.

The experience of an occasional, innocent flirting is like a good meal, an exceptional sunset, a symphony well played. They afford one pleasant memories.

You made me feel good because, when you were talking about yourself, I did not hear anything except the voice in my own mind. You see, I was really not interested in what you had to say. But what you said reminded me of another one of my own thoughts and that excited me and made me feel good.

Do you know what it takes to have friends?
Time.
Time to call, time to pay attention, time to
Listen, time to remember.
Friendship takes time and effort.
Effort to learn, to understand, to forgive, to build.
It takes time and effort and willingness.
Willingness to be a friend.
And it all takes time. Time, even when you don't have time
or want to make time, because that is what friendship really
is.....time.

℣ find that my focus on our relationship does not lie in you, but in what we create together by our relationship. The creation is, therefore, not the responsibility of one, you or me, but of our combined efforts, thus freeing each of the burden of the impossible, perfection.

It is interesting how all that talk about love and life and beauty and about people needing each other and about having great appreciation for the beautiful things in life makes so much sense when you are feeling good. But when you are depressed and lonely and in need of love and loving and being held close, all that seems so much talk. Curse the talk and the beautiful words and lovely thoughts. I need to be held and loved tenderly right now. I am lonely right now, and words don't fill the empty space......

Sometimes you are afraid that you are only taking from me, that you are taking advantage of me. That is not true. You feel that way when you are depressed and don't feel good about yourself. Then you cannot receive but only take. You do not take more than you have a right to take. But when you feel bad, you cannot receive what I have to give. There is a big difference between accepting what is given and taking what is needed. You feel the difference, but you can't explain it.

Lots of time and money is spent in looking at the past in order to smooth the way for the future. We would do well by directing more energy and love into the now, for the benefit of the future.

No matter which stand you take, you will always find someone who agrees with you and also someone who disagrees with you. You must take one step forward, let those two argue out their differences, while you make up your own mind as to what is right for you.

I looked at the wide sky last night
And tried to weigh my pain
Against all of life.
But it did not matter, the
Joys and suffering out there,
I still felt grief inside,
And inside of me was as full
And filling
As all of the outside was
Surrounding and
Extending.

I have stopped crying
And look on to you with a feeling of
Familiarity,
Of closeness,
Of belonging,
With love, yet with a feeling of eerie hollowness.
I stand quietly
And watch with a strange remoteness
As you go through your pain.
I should know what you are going through,
And yet I do not feel.
But I felt once.
It seems a long time ago now.
Time,
Oh God, yes, time.
It makes agony out of a single hurt,
Yet blesses us with a healing
When the agony eventually dulls
And is defused and thinned
And masked in the tapestry of life.

It is strange
How quiet everything gets
When a human being has confessed
To being in despair,
To being lost,
To being lonesome.
It is as if the whole world draws back
And looks on
Helplessly.
The sobbing echoes then for the whole world to hear.
One lonely person
In the multitude of the universe,
Pressing itself around him
Yet leaving him in a void,
Exposed,
Afraid,
Wondering why?
Wondering,
Where is everybody?

Summer is gone,
Autumn is here,
Time's gone by too fast
And I don't smile enough anymore.

I'll work this hard
A little while longer
And then I'm going to change,
Before the kids are gone,
Before the seasons change again, unnoticed,
Before time has gone by too fast.

I dreamt I walked across a field
With daisies in my hand.
The grass swayed gently in the wind,
The sun sent gold upon the land.

Then I saw you standing upon a hill
Beneath a black birch tree.
I waved and laughed and called your name.
You turned and looked at me.

I ran the hill and quite out of breath
Dumped daisies in your face.
Your eyes lit up, your hands reached out.
The flowers had found a place.

We sat together in the grass
And braided daisies in a string.
The time was filled with playful joy,
I the queen and you the king.

I saw your face, I saw your smile,
But next I did not understand.
You'd closed your eyes and behind your back
You had withdrawn your hand.

You'd let the string of daisies fall
And tears ran down your face.
You got up and moved away
And walked toward the birchtree place.

You stood again in that shaded spot
Your back against the tree.
And with a cloak held tightly 'round yourself
Your eyes, so sad, long looked at me.

The dream then ended and when I awoke
I was still holding daisies in my hand.
The bunch was somewhat smaller now
Though still woven in a strand.

Someday I hope I'll dream again
Of sitting next to you.
That you'll accept my string of blooms
If only just a few.

Because the daisies had brought you happiness
Once buried, guarded and deep.
But it's only with an open hand
That you can accept the ones to keep.

On the highway this morning an ambulance came up and everyone moved over. The red lights swirled, the siren screamed and I saw the cars move in groups out of the way. Yet is was more than the law that made people move over. It was that human response to an urgency, a cooperative response to a tragedy, it was the silent, awesome response to a command, "Move, someone is hurt." And the drivers helped as best they could.

The ambulance was the visible sign that someone was hurt. The cars moving over was a visible sign that each driver responded willingly and helpfully, and I choked up. I choked up because I, too, was hurt. But it wasn't visible. It was inside. I choked up because I wanted to be reached out to, also. I wanted someone to recognize my hurt. I wanted not to be alone. But I had no siren, and so I drove on and people took no notice, and I cried.

I thought peace, peace, peace,
And then I experienced it.

Yesterday I was depressed.
Someone asked me why, and I answered,
"Because of everything."

Today I feel great.
Someone asked me why, and I answered,
"Oh, because of everything."

Either everything changes or I do.

When I
Touch you or
Hug you or
Kiss you softly on your cheek,
It is not because I want to become
Intimate with you.
I touch you and
Hug you and
Kiss you softly,
Because I want to
Share with you feelings of
Tenderness,
Kindness and
Affection.

I love best when I feel loved.

To be loved by one or many
Is not enough
To erase the feeling of loneliness.
But to love just one in return,
Ah! That is life fulfilled.

My love for you is like laughter
Reflected in a thousand mirrors.

Tine Thevenin was born in the Netherlands and educated there and in the United States. In her twenties she received a BA degree in piano and music education and was flutist with the Florida Symphony Orchestra. In her thirties she became a La Leche League counselor and wrote and published *The Family Bed*, which has sold over 75,000 copies, appears in English, Dutch and German and was instrumental in reversing a 1987 Massachusetts criminal child abuse case. By 42 she was an accomplished tri-athlete and became the first woman to solo the grueling 500-mile Minnesota Border-to-Border Triathlon. In 1984 she became a winner in the International Toastmasters Speech Contest. In 1987 Tine received a personal invitation to be listed in *International Leaders In Achievement*, which will list "those who lead by example and whose philosophy of life has acted as a tremendous stimulus to others, particularly to the young of tomorrow." Her story has appeared in the *London Times*, the *New York Times*, as cover story for *Parents* magazine, and many other newspapers and journals from Australia to England, the USA to Bankok. She has twice appeared on the Phil Donahue Show and numerous other radio and television shows. Tine is a speaker, an international author, and a student of achievers. She now lives in Edina, Minnesota.

Ordering information:

The Family Bed: An Age-Old Concept In Childrearing, Avery Publishing Group, Garden City Park, N.Y.($9.45 pp)

Lake Harriet: The Unique History Of One Of The Most Beautiful Lakes In Minneapolis, Until 1925. (Currently out of print)

Crossing The Finish Line. On cassette tape. ($11.00pp)

Luck Is Not Butterfly ($10.95pp)

Order from:
Knudsen and Associates
6950 France Ave. South
Suite 107
Minneapolis, MN 55435

"I Love America" was the runner-up speech for the 1984 International Toastmasters Speech Contest.

"A Training Ride" appeared in *Tri-Athlete*, January 1986.

"The Silver Bell" appeared in *Mothering* magazine, Spring 1986.

"Stay With Me" appeared in *Mothering* magazine, Fall 1986.